Book 1
Python Programming
Professional Made Easy
BY SAM KEY

&

Book 2
MYSQL Programming
Professional Made Easy
BY SAM KEY

Book 1
Python Programming
Professional Made Easy
By Sam Key

Expert Python Programming Language Success in a Day for Any Computer User!

Programming Box Set #48: Python Programming Professional Made Easy & MYSQL Programming Professional Made Easy

Copyright 2015 by Sam Key - All rights reserved.

In no way is it legal to reproduce, duplicate, or transmit any part of this document in either electronic means or in printed format. Recording of this publication is strictly prohibited and any storage of this document is not allowed unless with written permission from the publisher. All rights reserved.

Programming Box Set #48: Python Programming Professional Made Easy &
MYSQL Programming Professional Made Easy

Table Of Contents

Introduction 5

Chapter 1 Introduction to Programming Languages 6

Chapter 2 Getting Prepped Up 8

Chapter 3 Statements 10

Chapter 4 Basic Operators – Part 1 12

Chapter 5 Basic Operators – Part 2 16

Chapter 6 Functions, Flow Control, and User Input 21

Conclusion 25

**Programming Box Set #48: Python Programming Professional Made Easy &
MYSQL Programming Professional Made Easy**

Introduction

I want to thank you and congratulate you for purchasing the book, "Python Programming Professional Made Easy: Expert Python Programming Language Success in a Day for Any Computer User!"

This book contains proven steps and strategies on how to program Python in a few days. The lessons ingrained here will serve as an introduction to the Python language and programming to you. With the little things you will learn here, you will still be able to create big programs.

The book is also designed to prepare you for advanced Python lessons. Make sure that you take note of all the pointers included here since they will help you a lot in the future.

Thanks again for purchasing this book. I hope you enjoy it!

Programming Box Set #48: Python Programming Professional Made Easy &
MYSQL Programming Professional Made Easy

Chapter 1: Introduction to Programming Languages

This short section is dedicated to complete beginners in programming. Knowing all the things included in this chapter will lessen the confusion that you might encounter while learning Python or any programming language.

Computers do not know or cannot do anything by itself. They just appear smart because of the programs installed on them.

Computer, Binary, or Machine Language

You cannot just tell a computer to do something using human language since they can only understand computer language, which is also called machine or binary language. This language only consists of 0's and 1's.

On the other hand, you may not know how to speak or write computer language. Even if you do, it will take you hours before you can tell a computer to do one thing since just one command may consist of hundreds or thousands of 1's and 0's. If you translate one letter in the human alphabet to them, you will get two or three 1's or 0's in return. Just imagine how many 1's and 0's you will need to memorize if you translate a sentence to computer language.

Assembly or Low Level Programming Language

In order to overcome that language barrier, programmers have developed assemblers. Assemblers act as translators between a human and a computer.

However, assemblers cannot comprehend human language. They can only translate binary language to assembly language and vice versa. So, in order to make use of assemblers, programmers need to learn their language, which is also called a low level language.

Unfortunately, assembly language is difficult to learn and memorize. Assembly language consists of words made from mnemonics that only computer experts know. And for one to just make the computer display something to the screen, a programmer needs to type a lot of those words.

High Level Programming Language

Another solution was developed, and that was high level programming languages such as C++, Java, and Python. High level programming languages act as a translator for humans and assembly language or humans to computer language.

Unlike assembly language (or low level language), high level programming languages are easier to understand since they commonly use English words instead of mnemonics. With it, you can also write shorter lines of codes since they already provide commonly used functions that are shortened into one or two keywords.

**Programming Box Set #48: Python Programming Professional Made Easy &
MYSQL Programming Professional Made Easy**

If you take one command or method in Python and translate it to assembly language, you will have long lines of codes. If you translate it to computer language, you will have thousands of lines composed of 1's and 0's.

In a nutshell, high level programming languages like Python are just translators for humans and computers to understand each other. In order for computers to do something for humans, they need to talk or instruct them via programming languages.

Many high level languages are available today. Among the rest, Python is one of the easiest languages to learn. In the next chapter, you will learn how to speak and write with Python language for your computer to do your bidding.

Programming Box Set #48: Python Programming Professional Made Easy & MYSQL Programming Professional Made Easy

Chapter 2: Getting Prepped Up

On the previous chapter, you have learned the purpose of programming languages. By choosing this book, you have already decided that Python is the language that you want to use to make your programs. In this chapter, your learning of speaking, writing, and using this language starts.

You, Python, and Your Computer

Before you start writing, take a moment to understand the relationship between you, the programming language, and the computer. Imagine that you are a restaurant manager, and you have hired two foreign guys to cook for the restaurant, which is the program you want to create. The diners in your restaurant are the users of your program.

The first guy is the chef who only knows one language that you do not know. He follows recipes to the letter, and he does not care if the recipe includes him jumping off the cliff. That guy is your computer.

The second guy is the chef's personal translator who will translate the language you speak or write, which is Python, to the language the chef knows. This translator is strict and does not tolerate typos in the recipes he translates. If he finds any mistake, he will tell it right to your face, walk away with the chef, and leave things undone.

He also does not care if the recipe tells the chef to run on circles until he dies. That is how they work. This guy is your programming language.

Since it is a hassle to tell them the recipe while they cook, you decided to write a recipe book instead. That will be your program's code that the translator will read to the chef.

Installing Python

You got two things to get to program in Python. First, get the latest release of Python. Go to this website: https://www.python.org/downloads/.

Download Python 3.4.2 or anything newer than that. Install it. Take note of the directory where you will install Python.

Once you are done with the installation, you must get a source code editor. It is recommended that you get Notepad++. If you already have a source code editor, no need to install Notepad++, too. To download Notepad++, go to: http://www.notepad-plus-plus.org/download/v6.6.9.html. Download and install it.

Version 2.x or 3.x

If you have already visited the Python website to download the program, you might have seen that there are two Python versions that you can download. As of

**Programming Box Set #48: Python Programming Professional Made Easy &
MYSQL Programming Professional Made Easy**

this writing, the first version is Python 3.4.2 and the second version is Python 2.7.8.

About that, it is best that you get the latest version, which is version 3.4.2. The latest version or build will be the only one getting updates and fixes. The 2.7.8 was already declared as the final release for the 2.x build.

Beginners should not worry about it. It is recommended that new Python programmers start with 3.x or later before thinking about exploring the older versions of Python.

Programming and Interactive Mode

Python has two modes. The first one is Programming and the second one is Interactive. You will be using the Interactive mode for the first few chapters of this book. On the other hand, you will be using the Programming mode on the last few chapters.

In Interactive mode, you can play around with Python. You can enter lines of codes on it, and once you press enter, Python will immediately provide a feedback or execute the code you input. To access Python's interactive mode, go to the directory where you installed Python and open the Python application. If you are running on Windows, just open the Run prompt, enter python, and click OK.

In Programming mode, you can test blocks of code in one go. Use a source editor to write the program. Save it as a .py file, and run it as Python program. In Windows, .py files will be automatically associated with Python after you install Python. Due to that, you can just double click the file, and it will run.

Chapter 3: Statements

A program's code is like a recipe book. A book contains chapters, paragraphs, and sentences. On the other hand, a program's code contains modules, functions, and statements. Modules are like chapters that contain the recipes for a full course meal. Procedures or functions are like paragraphs or sections that contain recipes. Statements are like the sentences or steps in a recipe. To code a program with Python, you must learn how to write statements.

Statements

Statements are the building blocks of your program. Each statement in Python contains one instruction that your computer will follow. In comparison to a sentence, statements are like imperative sentences, which are sentences that are used to issue commands or requests. Unlike sentences, Python, or programming languages in general, has a different syntax or structure.

For example, type the statement below on the interpreter:

print("Test")

Press the enter key. The interpreter will move the cursor to the next line and print 'Test' without the single quotes. The command in the sample statement is print. The next part is the details about the command the computer must do. In the example, it is ("test"). If you convert that to English, it is like you are commanding the computer to print the word Test on the program.

Python has many commands and each of them has unique purpose, syntax, and forms. For example, type this and press enter:

1 + 1

Python will return an answer, which is 2. The command there is the operator plus sign. The interpreter understood that you wanted to add the two values and told the computer to send the result of the operation.

Variables

As with any recipe, ingredients should be always present. In programming, there will be times that you would want to save some data in case you want to use them later in your program. And there is when variables come in.

Variables are data containers. They are the containers for your ingredients. You can place almost any type of data on them like numbers or text. You can change the value contained by a variable anytime. And you can use them anytime as long as you need them.

Programming Box Set #48: Python Programming Professional Made Easy & MYSQL Programming Professional Made Easy

To create one, all you need is to think of a name or identifier for the variable and assign or place a value to it. To create and assign a value to variables, follow the example below:

example1 = 10

On the left is the variable name. On the right is the value you want to assign to the variable. If you just want to create a variable, you can just assign 0 to the variable to act as a placeholder. In the middle is the assignment operator, which is the equal sign. That operator tells the interpreter that you want him to assign a value, which is on its right, to the name or object on the left.

To check if the variable example1 was created and it stored the value 10 in it, type the variable name on the interpreter and press enter. If you done it correctly, the interpreter will reply with the value of the variable. If not, it will reply with a NameError: name <variable_name> is not defined. It means that no variable with that name was created.

Take note, you cannot just create any name for a variable. You need to follow certain rules to avoid receiving syntax errors when creating them. And they are:

- Variable names should start with an underscore or a letter.
- Variable names must only contain letters, numbers, or underscores.
- Variable names can be one letter long or any length.
- Variable names must not be the same with any commands or reserved keywords in Python.
- Variable names are case sensitive. The variable named example1 is different from the variable named Example1.

As a tip, always use meaningful names for your variables. It will help you remember them easily when you are writing long lines of codes. Also, keep them short and use only one style of naming convention. For example, if you create a variable like thisIsAString make sure that you name your second variable like that too: thisIsTheSecondVariable not this_is_the_second_variable.

You can do a lot of things with variables. You can even assign expressions to them. By the way, expressions are combinations of numbers and/or variables together with operators that can be evaluated by the computer. For example:

Example1 = 10

Example2 = 5 + 19

Example3 = Example1 - Example2

If you check the value of those variables in the interpreter, you will get 10 for Example1, 24 for Example2, and -14 for Example3.

Programming Box Set #48: Python Programming Professional Made Easy & MYSQL Programming Professional Made Easy

Chapter 4: Basic Operators – Part 1

As of this moment, you have already seen three operators: assignment (=), addition (+), and subtraction (-) operators. You can use operators to process and manipulate the data and variables you have – just like how chefs cut, dice, and mix their ingredients.

Types of Python Operators

Multiple types of operators exist in Python. They are:

- Arithmetic
- Assignment
- Comparison
- Logical
- Membership
- Identity
- Bitwise

Up to this point, you have witnessed how arithmetic and assignment operators work. During your first few weeks of programming in Python, you will be also using comparison and logical operators aside from arithmetic and assignment operators. You will mostly use membership, identity, and bitwise later when you already advanced your Python programming skills.

As a reference, below is a list of operators under arithmetic and assignment. In the next chapter, comparison and logical will be listed and discussed briefly in preparation for later lessons.

For the examples that the list will use, x will have a value of 13 and y will have a value of 7.

Arithmetic

Arithmetic operators perform mathematical operations on numbers and variables that have numbers stored on them.

> **+ : Addition. Adds the values besides the operator.**

z = 13 + 7

z's value is equal to 20.

- : Subtraction. Subtracts the values besides the operator.

z = x – y

z's value is equal to 6.

* : Multiplication. Multiplies the values besides the operator.

z = x * y

z's value is equal to 91.

/ : Division. Divides the values besides the operator.

z = x / y

z's value is equal to 1.8571428571428572.

** : Exponent. Applies exponential power to the value to the left (base) with the value to the right (exponent).

z = x ** y

z's value is equal to 62748517.

// : Floor Division. Divides the values besides the operator and returns a quotient with removed digits after the decimal point.

z = x // y

z's value is equal to 1.

% : Modulus. Divides the values besides the operator and returns the remainder instead of the quotient.

z = x % y

z's value is equal to 6.

Assignment

Aside from the equal sign or simple assignment operator, other assignment operators exist. Mostly, they are combinations of arithmetic operators and the simple assignment operator.

They are used as shorthand methods when reassigning a value to a variable that is also included in the expression that will be assigned to it. Using them in your code simplifies and makes your statements clean.

= : Simple assignment operator. It assigns the value of the expression on its right hand side to the variable to its left hand side.

z = x + y * x − y % x

**Programming Box Set #48: Python Programming Professional Made Easy &
MYSQL Programming Professional Made Easy**

z's value is equal to 97.

The following assignment operators work like this: it applies the operation first on the value of the variable on its left and the result of the expression on its right. After that, it assigns the result of the operation to the variable on its left.

+= : Add and Assign

x += y

x's value is equal to 20. It is equivalent to x = x + y.

-= : Subtract and Assign

x -= y

x's value is equal to 6. It is equivalent to x = x – y.

*= : Multiply and assign

x *= y

x's value is equal to 91. It is equivalent to x = x * y.

/= : Divide and assign

x /= y

x's value is equal to 1.8571428571428572. It is equivalent to x = x / y.

**= : Exponent and Assign

x **= y

x's value is equal to 62748517. It is equivalent to x = x ** y.

//= : Floor Division and Assign

x //= y

x's value is equal to 1. It is equivalent to x = x // y.

%= : Modulus and Assign

x %= y

x's value is equal to 6. It is equivalent to x = x % y.

Programming Box Set #48: Python Programming Professional Made Easy &
MYSQL Programming Professional Made Easy

Multiple Usage of Some Operators

Also, some operators may behave differently depending on how you use them or what values you use together with them. For example:

z = "sample" + "statement"

As you can see, the statement tried to add two strings. In other programming languages, that kind of statement will return an error since their (+) operator is dedicated for addition of numbers only. In Python, it will perform string concatenation that will append the second string to the first. Hence, the value of variable z will become "samplestatement".

On the other hand, you can use the (-) subtraction operator as unary operators. To denote that a variable or number is negative, you can place the subtraction operator before it. For example:

z = 1 - -1

The result will be 2 since 1 minus negative 1 is 2.

The addition operator acts as a unary operator for other languages; however, it behaves differently in Python. In some language, an expression like this: +(-1), will be treated as positive 1. In Python, it will be treated as +1(-1), and if you evaluate that, you will still get negative 1.

To perform a unary positive, you can do this instead:

--1

In that example, Python will read it as −(-1) or -1 * -1 and it will return a positive 1.

Chapter 5: Basic Operators – Part 2

Operators seem to be such a big topic, right? You will be working with them all the time when programming in Python. Once you master or just memorize them all, your overall programming skills will improve since most programming languages have operators that work just like the ones in Python.

And just like a restaurant manager, you would not want to let your chef serve food with only unprocessed ingredients all the time. Not everybody wants salads for their dinner.

Comparison

Aside from performing arithmetic operations and storing values to variables, Python can also allow you to let the computer compare expressions. For example, you can ask your computer if 10 is greater than 20. Since 10 is greater than 20, it will reply with True – meaning the statement you said was correct. If you have compared 20 is greater than 10 instead, it will return a reply that says False.

== : Is Equal

z = x == y

z's value is equal to FALSE.

!= : Is Not Equal

z = x != y

z's value is equal to True.

> : Is Greater Than

z = x > y

z's value is equal to True.

< : Is Less Than

z = x < y

z's value is equal to FALSE.

>= : Is Greater Than or Equal

z = x >= y

z's value is equal to True.

Programming Box Set #48: Python Programming Professional Made Easy & MYSQL Programming Professional Made Easy

<= : Is Less Than or Equal

z = x <= y

z's value is equal to FALSE.

Note that the last two operators are unlike the combined arithmetic and simple assignment operator.

Logical

Aside from arithmetic and comparison operations, the computer is capable of logical operations, too. Even simple circuitry can do that, but that is another story to tell.

Anyway, do you remember your logic class where your professor talked about truth tables, premises, and propositions? Your computer can understand all of that. Below are the operators you can use to perform logic in Python. In the examples in the list, a is equal to True and b is equal to False.

and : Logical Conjunction AND. It will return only True both the propositions or variable besides it is True. It will return False if any or both the propositions are False.

w = a and a

x = a and b

y = b and a

z = b and b

w is equal to True, x is equal to False, y is equal to False, and z is equal to False.

or : Logical Disjunction OR. It will return True if any or both of the proposition or variable beside it is True. It will return False if both the propositions are False.

w = a or a

x = a or b

y = b or a

z = b or b

w is equal to True, x is equal to True, y is equal to True, and z is equal to False.

not : Logical Negation NOT. Any Truth value besides it will be negated. If True is negated, the computer will reply with a False. If False is negated, the computer will reply with a True.

w = not a

x = not b

w is equal to False and x is equal to True.

If you want to perform Logical NAND, you can use Logic Negation NOT and Logical Conjunction AND. For example:

w = not (a and a)

x = not (a and b)

y = not (b and a)

z = not (b and b)

w is equal to False, x is equal to True, y is equal to True, and z is equal to True.

If you want to perform Logical NOR, you can use Logic Negation NOT and Logical Disjunction OR. For example:

w = not (a or a)

x = not (a or b)

y = not (b or a)

z = not (b or b)

w is equal to False, x is equal to False, y is equal to False, and z is equal to True.

You can perform other logical operations that do not have Python operators by using conditional statements, which will be discussed later in this book.

Order of Precedence

In case that your statement contains multiple types or instances of operators, Python will evaluate it according to precedence of the operators, which is similar to the PEMDAS rule in Mathematics. It will evaluate the operators with the highest precedence to the lowest. For example:

z = 2 + 10 / 10

Programming Box Set #48: Python Programming Professional Made Easy & MYSQL Programming Professional Made Easy

Instead of adding 2 and 10 first then dividing the sum by 10, Python will divide 10 by 10 first then add 2 to the quotient instead since division has a higher precedence than subtraction. So, instead of getting 1.2, you will get 3.0. In case that it confuses you, imagine that Python secretly adds parentheses to the expression. The sample above is the same as:

z = 2 + (10 / 10)

If two operators with the same level of precedence exist in one statement, Python will evaluate the first operator that appears from the left. For example:

z = 10 / 10 * 2

The value of variable z will be 2.

Take note that any expressions inside parentheses or nested deeper in parentheses will have higher precedence than those expressions outside the parentheses. For example:

z = 2 / ((1 + 1) * (2 − 4))

Even though the division operator came first and has higher precedence than addition and subtraction, Python evaluated the ones inside the parentheses first and evaluated the division operation last. So, it added 1 and 1, subtracted 4 from 2, multiplied the sum and difference of the two previous operations, and then divided the product from 2. The value of variable z became -0.5.

Below is a reference for the precedence of the operations. The list is sorted from operations with high precedence to operators with low precedence.

- **Exponents**
- **Unary**
- **Multiplication, Division, Modulo, and Floor Division**
- **Addition, and Subtraction**
- **Bitwise**
- **Comparison**
- **Assignment**
- **Identity**
- **Membership**
- **Logical**

Truth Values

The values True and False are called truth values – or sometimes called Boolean data values. The value True is equal to 1 and the value False is equal to 0. That means that you can treat or use 1 as the truth value True and 0 as the truth value False. Try comparing those two values in your interpreter. Code the following:

Programming Box Set #48: Python Programming Professional Made Easy & MYSQL Programming Professional Made Easy

True == 1

False == 0

The interpreter will return a value of True – meaning, you can interchange them in case a situation arises. However, it is advisable that that you use them like that sparingly.

Another thing you should remember is that the value True and False are case sensitive. True != TRUE or False != false. Aside from that, True and False are Python keywords. You cannot create variables named after them.

You might be wondering about the use of truth values in programming. The answer is, you can use them to control your programs using conditional or flow control tools. With them, you can make your program execute statements when a certain condition arises. And that will be discussed on the next chapter.

Programming Box Set #48: Python Programming Professional Made Easy &
MYSQL Programming Professional Made Easy

Chapter 6: Functions, Flow Control, and User Input

With statements, you have learned to tell instructions to the computer using Pythons. As of now, all you know is how to assign variables and manipulate expressions. And the only command you know is print. Do you think you can make a decent program with those alone? Maybe, but you do not need to rack your brains thinking of one.

In this chapter, you will learn about functions and flow control. This time, you will need to leave the interpreter or Interactive mode. Open your source code editor since you will be programming blocks of codes during this section.

Functions

Statements are like sentences in a book or steps in a recipe. On the other hand, functions are like paragraphs or a recipe in a recipe book. Functions are blocks of code with multiple statements that will perform a specific goal or goals when executed. Below is an example:

def recipe1():

    print("Fried Fish Recipe")

    print("Ingredients:")

    print("Fish")

    print("Salt")

    print("Steps:")

    print("1. Rub salt on fish.")

    print("2. Fry fish.")

    print("3. Serve.")

The function's purpose is to print the recipe for Fried Fish. To create a function, you will need to type the keyword def (for define) then the name of the function. In the example, the name of the function is recipe1. The parentheses are important to be present there. It has its purpose, but for now, leave it alone.

After the parentheses, a colon was placed. The colon signifies that a code block will be under the function.

To include statements inside that code block, you must indent it. In the example, one indentation or tab was used. To prevent encountering errors, make sure that all the statements are aligned and have the same number of indentations.

Programming Box Set #48: Python Programming Professional Made Easy & MYSQL Programming Professional Made Easy

To end the code block for the function, all you need is to type a statement that has the same indentation level of the function declaration.

By the way, all the statements inside a function code block will not be executed until the function is called or invoked. To invoke the function, all you need is to call it using its name. To invoke the function recipe1, type this:

recipe1()

And that is how simple functions work.

Flow Control

It is sad that only one recipe can be displayed by the sample function. It would be great if your program can display more recipes. And letting the user choose the recipe that they want to be displayed on the program would be cool. But how can you do that?

You can do that by using flow control tools in Python. With them, you can direct your program to do something if certain conditions are met. In the case of the recipe listing program, you can apply flow control and let them see the recipes by requesting it.

If Statement

The simplest control flow tool you can use for this type of project is the if statement. Have you been wondering about truth values? Now, you can use them with if statements.

An *if statement* is like a program roadblock. If the current condition of your program satisfies its requirements, then it will let it access the block of statements within it. It is like a function with no names, and instead of being invoked to work, it needs you to satisfy the conditions set to it. For example:

a = 2

if a == 2:

    print("You satisfied the condition!")

    print("This is another statement that will be executed!")

if a == (1 + 1):

    print("You satisfied the condition again!")

    print("I will display the recipe for Fried Fish!")

    recipe1()

Programming Box Set #48: Python Programming Professional Made Easy & MYSQL Programming Professional Made Easy

If you will translate the first if statement in English, it will mean that: if variable a is equals to 2, then print the sentence inside the parentheses. Another way to translate it is: if the comparison between variable a and the number 2 returns True, then print the sentence inside the parentheses.

As you can see, the colon is there and the statements below the if statement are indented, too. It really is like a function.

User Input

You can now control the flow of your program and create functions. Now, about the recipe program, how can the user choose the recipe he wants to view? That can be done by using the input() command. You can use it like this:

a = input("Type your choice here and press enter: ")

Once Python executes that line, it will stop executing statements. And provide a prompt that says "Type your choice here: ". During that moment, the user will be given a chance to type something in the program. If the user press enter, Python will store and assign the characters the user typed on the program to variable a. Once that process is done, Python will resume executing the statements after the input statement.

In some cases, programmers use the input command to pause the program and wait for the user to press enter. You can do that by just placing input() on a line.

With that, you can make a program that can capture user input and can change its flow whenever it gets the right values from the user. You can create a recipe program that allows users to choose the recipe they want. Here is the code. Analyze it. And use the things you have learned to improve it. Good luck.

print("Enter the number of the recipe you want to read.")

print("1 - Fried Fish")

print("2 - Fried Egg")

print("Enter any character to Exit")

choice = input("Type a Number and Press Enter: ")

if choice == "1":

    print("Fried Fish Recipe")

    print("Ingredients:")

    print("Fish")

```python
        print("Salt")

        print("Steps:")

        print("1. Rub salt on fish.")

        print("2. Fry fish.")

        print("3. Serve.")

        pause = input("Press enter when you are done reading.")


if choice == "2":

        print("Fried Egg Recipe")

        print("Ingredients:")

        print("Egg")

        print("Salt")

        print("Steps:")

        print("1. Fry egg.")

        print("2. Sprinkle Salt.")

        print("3. Serve.")

        pause = input("Press enter when you are done reading.")
```

Programming Box Set #48: Python Programming Professional Made Easy & MYSQL Programming Professional Made Easy

Conclusion

Thank you again for purchasing this book!

I hope this book was able to help you to learn the basics of Python programming.

The next step is to learn more about Python! You should have expected that coming.

Kidding aside, with the current knowledge you have in Python programming, you can make any programs like that with ease. But of course, there are still lots of things you need to learn about the language such as loops, classes, and etcetera.

Finally, if you enjoyed this book, please take the time to share your thoughts and post a review on Amazon. We do our best to reach out to readers and provide the best value we can. Your positive review will help us achieve that. It'd be greatly appreciated!

Thank you and good luck!

Book 2
MYSQL Programming
Professional Made Easy

By Sam Key

Expert MYSQL Programming Language Success in a Day for any Computer User!

Programming Box Set #48: Python Programming Professional Made Easy & MYSQL Programming Professional Made Easy

Copyright 2015 by Sam Key - All rights reserved.

In no way is it legal to reproduce, duplicate, or transmit any part of this document in either electronic means or in printed format. Recording of this publication is strictly prohibited and any storage of this document is not allowed unless with written permission from the publisher. All rights reserved.

Programming Box Set #48: Python Programming Professional Made Easy & MYSQL Programming Professional Made Easy

Table Of Contents

Introduction 29

Chapter 1: Introduction to MySQL 30

Chapter 2: Database and SQL 31

Chapter 3: SQL Syntax 33

Chapter 4: SQL Keywords, Clauses, and Statements 35

Chapter 5: MySQL and PHP 43

Conclusion 47

Check Out My Other Books 48

Programming Box Set #48: Python Programming Professional Made Easy & MYSQL Programming Professional Made Easy

Introduction

I want to thank you and congratulate you for purchasing the book, "MYSQL Programming Professional Made Easy: Expert MYSQL Programming Language Success in a Day for any Computer User!".

This book contains proven steps and strategies on how to manage MySQL databases.

The book will teach you the fundamentals of SQL and how to apply it on MySQL. It will cover the basic operations such as creating and deleting tables and databases. Also, it will tell you how to insert, update, and delete records in MySQL. In the last part of the book, you will be taught on how to connect to your MySQL server and send queries to your database using PHP.

Thankfully, by this time, this subject is probably a piece of cake for you since you might already have experienced coding in JavaScript and PHP, which are prerequisites to learning MySQL.

However, it does not mean that you will have a difficult time learning MySQL if you do not have any idea on those two scripting languages. In this book, you will learn about SQL, which works a bit different from programming languages.

Being knowledgeable alone with SQL can give you a solid idea on how MySQL and other RDBMS work. Anyway, thanks again for purchasing this book, I hope you enjoy it!

Programming Box Set #48: Python Programming Professional Made Easy & MYSQL Programming Professional Made Easy

Chapter 1: Introduction to MySQL

This book will assume that you are already knowledgeable about PHP. It will focus on database application on the web. The examples here will use PHP as the main language to use to access a MySQL database. Also, this will be focused on Windows operating system users.

As of now, MySQL is the most popular database system by PHP programmers. Also, it is the most popular database system on the web. A few of the websites that use MySQL to store their data are Facebook, Wikipedia, and Twitter.

Commonly, MySQL databases are ran on web servers. Because of that, you need to use a server side scripting language to use it.

A few of the good points of MySQL against other database systems are it is scalable (it is good to use in small or large scale applications), fast, easy to use, and reliable. Also, if you are already familiar with SQL, you will not have any problems in manipulating MySQL databases.

Preparation

In the first part of this book, you will learn SQL or Standard Query Language. If you have a database program, such as Microsoft Access, installed in your computer, you can use it to practice and apply the statements you will learn.

In case you do not, you have two options. Your first option is to get a hosting account package that includes MySQL and PHP. If you do not want to spend tens of dollars for a paid web hosting account, you can opt for a free one. However, be informed that most of them will impose limitations or add annoyances, such as ads, in your account. Also, some of them have restrictions that will result to your account being banned once you break one of them.

Your second option is to get XAMMP, a web server solution that includes Apache, MySQL, and PHP. It will turn your computer into a local web server. And with it, you can play around with your MySQL database and the PHP codes you want to experiment with. Also, it comes with phpMyAdmin. A tool that will be discussed later in this book.

Programming Box Set #48: Python Programming Professional Made Easy & MYSQL Programming Professional Made Easy

Chapter 2: Database and SQL

What is a database? A database is an application or a file wherein you can store data. It is used and included in almost all types of computer programs. A database is usually present in the background whether the program is a game, a word processor, or a website.

A database can be a storage location for a player's progress and setting on a game. It can be a storage location for dictionaries and preferences in word processors. And it can be a storage location for user accounts and page content in websites.

There are different types and forms of databases. A spreadsheet can be considered a database. Even a list of items in a text file can be considered one, too. However, unlike the database that most people know or familiar with, those kinds of databases are ideal for small applications.

RDBMS

The type of database that is commonly used for bigger applications is RDBMS or relational database management system. MySQL is an RDBMS. Other RDBMS that you might have heard about are Oracle database, Microsoft Access, and SQL Server.

Inside an RDBMS, there are tables that are composed of rows, columns, and indexes. Those tables are like spreadsheets. Each cell in a table holds a piece of data. Below is an example table:

username	password	email	firstname	lastname
Johnnyxxx	123abc	jjxxx@gmail.com	Johnny	Stew
cutiepatutie	qwertyuiop	cuteme@yahoo.com	Sara	Britch
mastermiller	theGear12	mgshades@gmail.com	Master	Miller
j_sasaki	H9fmaNCa	j_sasaki@gmail.com	Johnny	Sasaki

**Programming Box Set #48: Python Programming Professional Made Easy &
MYSQL Programming Professional Made Easy**

Note: this same table will be used as the main reference of all the examples in this book. Also, developers usually encrypt their passwords in their databases. They are not encrypted for the sake of an example.

In the table, which the book will refer to as the account table under the sample database, there are six columns (or fields) and they are id, username, password, email, firstname, and lastname. As of now, there are only four rows. Rows can be also called entries or records. Take note that the first row is not part of the count. They are just there to represent the name of the columns as headers.

An RDBMS table can contain one or more tables.

Compared to other types of databases, RDBMS are easier to use and manage because it comes with a standardized set of method when it comes to accessing and manipulating data. And that is SQL or Standard Query Language.

SQL

Before you start learning MySQL, you must familiarize yourself with SQL or Standard Query Language first. SQL is a language used to manipulate and access relational database management systems. It is not that complicated compared to learning programming languages.

Few of the things you can do with databases using SQL are:

- Get, add, update, and delete data from databases
- Create, modify, and delete databases
- Modify access permissions in databases

Most database programs use SQL as the standard method of accessing databases, but expect that some of them have a bit of variations. Some statements have different names or keywords while some have different methods to do things. Nevertheless, most of the usual operations are the same for most of them.

A few of the RDBMS that you can access using SQL – with little alterations – are MySQL, SQL Server, and Microsoft Access.

Programming Box Set #48: Python Programming Professional Made Easy &
MYSQL Programming Professional Made Easy

Chapter 3: SQL Syntax

SQL is like a programming language. It has its own set of keywords and syntax rules. Using SQL is like talking to the database. With SQL, you can pass on commands to the database in order for it to present and manipulate the data it contains for you. And you can do that by passing queries and statements to it.

SQL is commonly used interactively in databases. As soon as you send a query or statement, the database will process it immediately. You can perform some programming in SQL, too. However, it is much easier to leave the programming part to other programming languages. In the case of MySQL, it is typical that most of the programming is done with PHP, which is the most preferred language to use with it.

SQL's syntax is simple. Below is an example:

SELECT username FROM account

In the example, the query is commanding the database to get all the data under the username column from the account table. The database will reply with a recordset or a collection of records.

In MySQL, databases will also return the number of rows it fetched and the duration that it took to fetch the result.

Case Sensitivity

As you can see, the SQL query is straightforward and easy to understand. Also, take note that unlike PHP, MySQL is not case sensitive. Even if you change the keyword SELECT's case to select, it will still work. For example:

seLeCT username from account

However, as a standard practice, it is best that you type keywords on uppercase and values in lowercase.

Line Termination

In case that you will perform or send consecutive queries or a multiline query, you need to place a semicolon at the end of each statement to separate them. By the way, MySQL does not consider a line to be a statement when it sees a new line character – meaning, you can place other parts of your queries on multiple lines. For example:

SELECT

Programming Box Set #48: Python Programming Professional Made Easy & MYSQL Programming Professional Made Easy

username

FROM

account;

New lines are treated like a typical whitespace (spaces and tabs) character. And the only accepted line terminator is a semicolon. In some cases, semicolons are not needed to terminate a line.

Programming Box Set #48: Python Programming Professional Made Easy & MYSQL Programming Professional Made Easy

Chapter 4: SQL Keywords and Statements

When you memorize the SQL keywords, you can say that you are already know SQL or MySQL. Truth be told, you will be mostly using only a few SQL keywords for typical database management. And almost half of the queries you will be making will be SELECT queries since retrieving data is always the most used operation in databases.

Before you learn that, you must know how to create a database first.

CREATE DATABASE

Creating a database is simple. Follow the syntax below:

CREATE DATABASE <name of database>;

To create the sample database where the account table is located, this is all you need to type:

CREATE DATABASE sample;

Easy, right? However, an empty database is a useless database. You cannot enter any data to it yet since you do not have tables yet.

CREATE TABLE

Creating a table requires a bit of planning. Before you create a table, you must already know the columns you want to include in it. Also, you need to know the size, type, and other attributes of the pieces of data that you will insert on your columns. Once you do, follow the syntax below:

CREATE TABLE <name of table>

(

<name of column 1> <data type(size)> <attributes>,

<name of column 2> <data type(size)> <attributes>,

<name of column 3> <data type(size)> <attributes>

);

Programming Box Set #48: Python Programming Professional Made Easy & MYSQL Programming Professional Made Easy

By the way, you cannot just create a table out of nowhere. To make sure that the table you will create will be inside a database, you must be connected to one. Connection to databases will be discussed in the later part of this book. As of now, imagine that you are now connected to the sample database that was just created in the previous section.

To create the sample account table, you need to do this:

CREATE TABLE account

(

id int(6) PRIMARY KEY UNSIGNED AUTO_INCREMENT PRIMARY KEY,

username varchar(16),

password varchar(16),

email varchar(32),

firstname var(16),

lastname var(16),

);

The example above commands the database to create a table named account. Inside the parentheses, the columns that will be created inside the account table are specified. They are separated with a comma. The first column that was created was the id column.

According to the example, the database needs to create the id column (id). It specified that the type of data that it will contain would be integers with six characters (int(6)). Also, it specified some optional attributes. It said that the id column will be the PRIMARY KEY of the table and its values will AUTO_INCREMENT – these will be discussed later. Also, it specified that the integers or data under it will be UNSIGNED, which means that only positive integers will be accepted.

MySQL Data Types

As mentioned before, databases or RDBMS accept multiple types of data. To make databases clean, it is required that you state the data type that you will input in your table's columns. Aside from that, an RDBMS also needs to know the size of the data that you will enter since it will need to allocate the space it needs to store the data you will put in it. Providing precise information about the size of your data will make your database run optimally.

**Programming Box Set #48: Python Programming Professional Made Easy &
MYSQL Programming Professional Made Easy**

Below are some of the data types that you will and can store in a MySQL database:

- INT(size) – integer data type. Numbers without fractional components or decimal places. A column with an INT data type can accept any number between -2147483648 to 2147483648. In case that you specified that it will be UNSIGNED, the column will accept any number between 0 to 4294967295. You can specify the number of digits with INT. The maximum is 11 digits – it will include the negative sign (-).
- FLOAT(size, decimal) – float data type. Numbers with fractional components or decimal places. It cannot be UNSIGNED. You can specify the number of digits it can handle and the number of decimal places it will store. If you did not specify the size and number of decimals, MySQL will set it to 10 digits and 2 decimal places (the decimal places is included in the count of the digits). Float can have the maximum of 24 digits.
- TIME – time will be stored and formatted as HH:MM:SS.
- DATE – date will be stored and formatted as YYYY-MM-DD. It will not accept any date before year 1,000. And it will not accept date that exceeds 31 days and 12 months.
- DATETIME – combination of DATE and TIME formatted as YYYY-MM-DD HH:MM:SS.
- TIMESTAMP – formatted differently from DATETIME. Its format is YYYYMMDDHHMMSS. It can only store date and time between 19700101000000 and 20371231235959 (not accurate).
- CHAR(size) – stores strings with fixed size. It can have a size of 1 to 255 characters. It uses static memory allocation, which makes it perform faster than VARCHAR. It performs faster because the database will just multiply its way to reach the location of the data you want instead of searching every byte to find the data that you need. To make the data fixed length, it is padded with spaces after the last character.
- VARCHAR(size) – stores strings with variable length size. It can have a size of 1 to 255 characters. It uses dynamic memory allocation, which is slower than static. However, when using VARCHAR, it is mandatory to specify the data's size.
- BLOB –store BLOBs (Binary Large Objects). Data is stored as byte strings instead of character strings (in contrast to TEXT). This makes it possible to store images, documents, or other files in the database.
- TEXT – store text with a length of 65535 characters or less.
- ENUM(x, y, z) – with this, you can specify the values that can be only stored.

INT, BLOB, and TEXT data types can be set smaller or bigger. For example, you can use TINYINT instead of INT to store smaller data. TINYINT can only hold values ranging from -128 to 127 compared to INT that holds values ranging from -2147483648 to 2147483647.

The size of the data type ranges from TINY, SMALL, MEDIUM, NORMAL, and BIG.

- TINYINT, SMALLINT, MEDIUMINT, INT, and BIGINT
- TINYBLOB, SMALLBLOB, MEDIUMBLOB, BLOB, and BIGBLOB
- TINYTEXT, SMALLTEXT, MEDIUMTEXT, TEXT, and BIGTEXT

You already know how to create databases and tables. Now, you need to learn how to insert values inside those tables.

INSERT INTO and VALUES

There are two ways to insert values in your database. Below is the syntax for the first method:

INSERT INTO <name of table>

VALUES (<value 1>, <value 2>, <value 3>);

The same result be done by:

INSERT INTO <name of table>

(<column 1>, <column 2>, <column 3>)

VALUES (<value 1>, <value 2>, <value 3>);

Take note that the first method will assign values according to the arrangement of your columns in the tables. In case you do not want to enter a data to one of the columns in your table, you will be forced to enter an empty value.

On the other hand, if you want full control of the INSERT operation, it will be much better to indicate the name of the corresponding columns that will be given data. Take note that the database will assign the values you will write with respect of the arrangement of the columns in your query.

For example, if you want to insert data in the example account table, you need to do this:

INSERT INTO account

(username, password, email, firstname, lastname)

Programming Box Set #48: Python Programming Professional Made Easy & MYSQL Programming Professional Made Easy

VALUES

("Johnnyxxx", "123abc", "jjxxx@gmail.com", "Johnny", "Stew");

The statement will INSERT one entry to the database. You might have noticed that the example did not include a value for the ID field. You do not need to do that since the ID field has the AUTO_INCREMENT attribute. The database will be the one to generate a value to it.

SELECT and FROM

To check if the entry you sent was saved to the database, you can use SELECT. As mentioned before, the SELECT statement will retrieve all the data that you want from the database. Its syntax is:

SELECT <column 1> FROM <name of table>;

If you use this in the example account table and you want to get all the usernames in it, you can do it by:

SELECT username FROM account;

In case that you want to multiple records from two or more fields, you can do that by specifying another column. For example:

SELECT username, email FROM account;

WHERE

Unfortunately, using SELECT alone will provide you with tons of data. And you do not want that all the time. To filter out the results you want or to specify the data you want to receive, you can use the WHERE clause. For example:

SELECT <column 1> FROM <name of table>

WHERE <column> <operator> <value>;

If ever you need to get the username of all the people who have Johnny as their first name in the account table, you do that by:

SELECT username FROM account

WHERE firstname = "Johnny";

In the query above, the database will search all the records in the username column that has the value Johnny on the firstname column. The query will return Johnnyxxx and j_sasaki.

LIMIT

What if you only need a specific number of records to be returned? You can use the LIMIT clause for that. For example:

SELECT <column 1> FROM <name of table>

LIMIT <number>;

If you only want one record from the email column to be returned when you use SELECT on the account table, you can do it by:

SELECT email FROM account

LIMIT 1;

You can use the LIMIT clause together with the WHERE clause for you to have a more defined search. For example:

SELECT username FROM account

WHERE firstname = "Johnny"

LIMIT 1;

Instead of returning two usernames that have Johnny in the firstname field, it will only return one.

UPDATE and SET

What if you made a mistake and you want to append an entry on your table? Well, you can use UPDATE for that. For example:

UPDATE <name of table>

SET <column 1>=<value 1>, <column 1>=<value 1>, <column 1>=<value 1>

WHERE <column> <operator> <value>;

Programming Box Set #48: Python Programming Professional Made Easy & MYSQL Programming Professional Made Easy

In the example account table, if you want to change the name of all the people named Master to a different one, you can do that by:

UPDATE account

SET firstname="David"

WHERE firstname="Master";

Take note, you can perform an UPDATE without the WHERE clause. However, doing so will make the database think that you want to UPDATE all the records in the table. Remember that it is a bit complex to ROLLBACK changes in MySQL, so be careful.

DELETE

If you do not to remove an entire row, you can use DELETE. However, if you just want to delete or remove one piece of data in a column, it is better to use UPDATE and place a blank value instead. To perform a DELETE, follow this syntax:

DELETE FROM <name of table>

WHERE <column> <operator> <value>;

If you want to delete the first row in the account table, do this:

DELETE FROM account

WHERE id = 1;

Just like with the UPDATE statement, make sure that you use the WHERE clause when using DELETE. If not, all the rows in your table will disappear.

TRUNCATE TABLE

If you just want to remove all the data inside your table and keep all the settings that you have made to it you need to use TRUNCATE TABLE. This is the syntax for it:

TRUNCATE TABLE <name of table>;

If you want to do that to the account table, do this by entering:

TRUNCATE TABLE account;

DROP TABLE and DROP DATABASE

Finally, if you want to remove a table or database, you can use DROP. Below are examples on how to DROP the account table and sample database.

DROP TABLE account;

DROP DATABASE sample;

Programming Box Set #48: Python Programming Professional Made Easy &
MYSQL Programming Professional Made Easy

Chapter 5: MySQL and PHP

You already know how to manage a MySQL server to the most basic level. Now, it is time to use all those statements and use PHP to communicate with the MySQL server.

To interact or access a MySQL database, you need to send SQL queries to it. There are multiple ways you can do that. But if you want to do it in the web or your website, you will need to use a server side scripting language. And the best one to use is PHP.

In PHP, you can communicate to a MySQL server by using PDO (PHP Data Objects), MySQL extension, or MySQLi extension. Compared to MySQLi extension, PDO is a better choice when communicating with a MySQL database. However, in this book, only MySQLi extension will be discussed since it is less complex and easier to use.

Connecting to a MySQL database:

Before you can do or say anything to a MySQL server or a database, you will need to connect to it first. To do that, follow this example:

```php
<?php
$dbservername = "localhost";
$dbusername = "YourDataBaseUserName";
$dbpassword = "YourPassword12345";

// Create a new connection object
$dbconnection = new mysqli($dbservername, $ dbusername, $ dbpassword);

// Check if connection was successful
if ($dbconnection->connect_error) {
    die("Connection failed/error: " . $dbconnection->connect_error);
}
echo "Connected successfully to database";
?>
```

In this example, you are using PHP's MySQLi to connect to your database. If you are going to test the code in the server that you installed in your computer, use localhost for your database's server name.

By the way, to prevent hackers on any random internet surfers to edit or access your databases, your MySQL server will require you to set a username and password. Every time you connect to it, you will need to include it to the parameters of the mysqli object.

Programming Box Set #48: Python Programming Professional Made Easy & MYSQL Programming Professional Made Easy

In the example, you have created an object under the mysqli class. All the information that the server will send to you will be accessible in this object.

The third block of code is used to check if your connection request encountered any trouble. As you can see, the if statement is checking whether the connect_error property of the object $dbconnection contains a value. If it does, the code will be terminated and return an error message.

On the other hand, if the connect_error is null, the code will proceed and echo a message that will tell the user that the connection was successful.

Closing a connection

To close a mysqli object's connection, just invoke its close() method. For example:

$dbconnection->close();

Creating a new MySQL Database

```
<?php
$dbservername = "localhost";
$dbusername = "YourDataBaseUserName";
$dbpassword = "YourPassword12345";

// Create a new connection object
$dbconnection = new mysqli($dbservername, $ dbusername, $ dbpassword);

// Check if connection was successful
if ($dbconnection->connect_error) {
    die("Connection failed/error: " . $dbconnection->connect_error);
}


// Creating a Database

$dbSQL = "CREATE DATABASE YourDatabaseName";

if ($dbconnection->query($dbSQL) === TRUE) {

      echo "YourDatabaseName was created.";

}
else {

      echo "An error was encountered while creating your database: " . $dbconnection->error;

}
```

```
$dbconnection->close();
?>
```

Before you request a database to be created, you must connect to your MySQL server first. Once you establish a connection, you will need to tell your server to create a database by sending an SQL query.

The $dbSQL variable was created to hold the query string that you will send. You do not need to do this, but creating a variable for your queries is good practice since it will make your code more readable. If you did not create a variable holder for your SQL, you can still create a database by:

```
$dbconnection->query("CREATE DATABASE YourDatabaseName")
```

The if statement was used to both execute the query method of $dbconnection and to check if your server will be able to do it. If it does, it will return a value of TRUE. The if statement will inform you that you were able to create your database.

On the other hand, if it returns false or an error instead, the example code will return a message together with the error.

Once the database was created, the connection was closed.

Interacting with a Database

Once you create a database, you can now send SQL queries and do some operations in it. Before you do that, you need to connect to the server and then specify the name of the database, which you want to interact with, in the parameters of the mysqli class when creating a mysqli object. For example:

```
<?php
$dbservername = "localhost";
$dbusername = "YourDataBaseUserName";
$dbpassword = "YourPassword12345";

$dbname = "sample"

// Create a new connection object
$dbconnection = new mysqli($dbservername, $ dbusername, $ dbpassword, $sample);

// Check if connection was successful
if ($dbconnection->connect_error) {
    die("Connection failed/error: " . $dbconnection->connect_error);
}
echo "Connected successfully to database";
?>
```

**Programming Box Set #48: Python Programming Professional Made Easy &
MYSQL Programming Professional Made Easy**

phpMyAdmin

In case you do not want to rely on code to create and manage your databases, you can use the phpMyAdmin tool. Instead of relying on sending SQL queries, you will be given a user interface that is easier to use and reduces the chances of error since you do not need to type SQL and create typos. Think of it as Microsoft Access with a different interface.

The tool will also allow you to enter SQL if you want to and it will provide you with the SQL queries that it has used to perform the requests you make. Due to that, this tool will help you get more familiar with SQL. And the best thing about it is that it is free.

On the other hand, you can use phpMyAdmin to check the changes you made to the database while you are studying MySQL. If you do that, you will be able to debug faster since you do not need to redisplay or create a code for checking the contents of your database using PHP.

Programming Box Set #48: Python Programming Professional Made Easy & MYSQL Programming Professional Made Easy

Conclusion

Thank you again for purchasing this book!

I hope this book was able to help you to master the fundamentals of MySQL programming.

The next step is to learn more about:

- Advanced SQL Statements and Clauses
- Attributes
- The MySQLi Class
- PHP Data Object
- Security Measures in MySQL
- Importing and Exporting MySQL Databases
- Different Applications of MySQL

Those topics will advance your MySQL programming skills. Well, even with the things you have learned here, you will already be capable of doing great things. With the knowledge you have, you can already create an online chat application, social network site, and online games!

That is no exaggeration. If you do not believe that, well, check out the sample codes that experts share on the web. You will be surprised how simple their codes are.

Finally, if you enjoyed this book, please take the time to share your thoughts and post a review on Amazon. We do our best to reach out to readers and provide the best value we can. Your positive review will help us achieve that. It'd be greatly appreciated!

Thank you and good luck!

Programming Box Set #48: Python Programming Professional Made Easy & MYSQL Programming Professional Made Easy

Check Out My Other Books

Below you'll find some of my other popular books that are popular on Amazon and Kindle as well. Simply click on the links below to check them out. Alternatively, you can visit my author page on Amazon to see other work done by me.

Android Programming in a Day

Python Programming in a Day

C Programming Success in a Day

C Programming Professional Made Easy

JavaScript Programming Made Easy

PHP Programming Professional Made Easy

C ++ Programming Success in a Day

Windows 8 Tips for Beginners

HTML Professional Programming Made Easy

If the links do not work, for whatever reason, you can simply search for these titles on the Amazon website to find them.

Printed in Great Britain
by Amazon